Super Heroes Crochet Ideas

Amazing Super Hero Pattern To Try This Weekend

Copyright © 2021

All rights reserved.

DEDICATION

The author and publisher have provided this e-book to you for your personal use only. You may not make this e-book publicly available in any way. Copyright infringement is against the law. If you believe the copy of this e-book you are reading infringes on the author's copyright, please notify the publisher at: https://us.macmillan.com/piracy

Contents

Groot 1

Spider Man 17

The Flash 27

Doctor Strange 39

Batman and Robin 61

Robin the Boy Wonder 67

Wonder Woman 73

Loki 82

Deadpool 95

Super Heroes Crochet Ideas

Groot

Super Heroes Crochet Ideas

What You'll Need

– H8/5.00mm and F5/3.5mm crochet hooks

– Worsted weight yarn in Brown (I used Rowan Summer Tweed in Chocolate Fudge, but it's discontinued now. I believe Lion Brand Vanna's Choice has a brown tweed, and Plymouth Encore Worsted definitely has a brown tweed, but any brown or tan/wood color will work!)

– Sport weight yarn in Green (I used Red Heart Designer Sport in Pistachio)

– Black embroidery thread or Black worsted weight yarn (I used Lion Brand Vanna's Choice in Black) – If you'd rather not crochet tiny leaves, you can also use green felt to cut out leaves, and sew them on with green or brown thread.

– 2 9mm safey eyes (12mm looks cute, too!)

– small amount of Polyfil

– 1 12-inch pipe cleaner or some kind of wire for the arms

– scissors

– tapestry needle

– small plant pot

– a handful of small, smooth pebbles

– optional: fake moss, hot glue

Abbreviations

ch(s): chain(s)

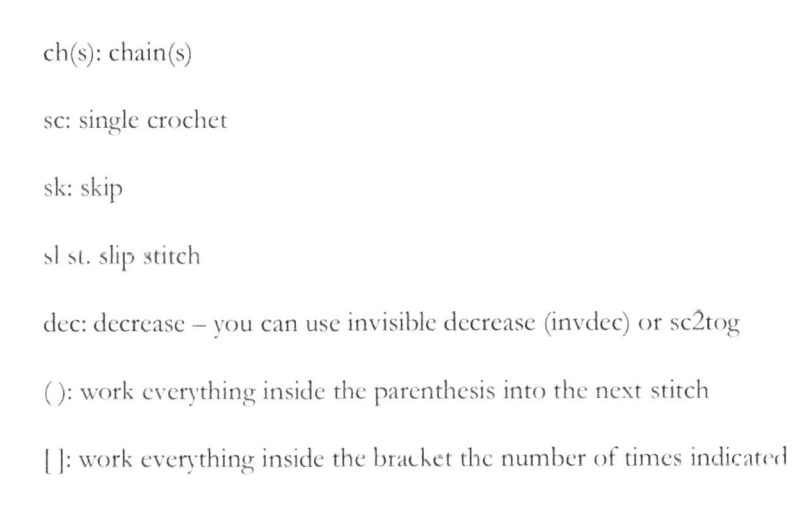

sc: single crochet

sk: skip

sl st. slip stitch

dec: decrease – you can use invisible decrease (invdec) or sc2tog

( ): work everything inside the parenthesis into the next stitch

[ ]: work everything inside the bracket the number of times indicated

Notes

I just busted out this pattern last night, and it has not been tested yet. If there are any booboos or weird spots, let me know!

Head Part A

With Brown and H hook, make magic ring, or ch 3 and sl st to 1st ch to form ring.

Rnd 1: Ch 1, 6 sc into ring. (6) Don't join rnds. Continue to work in a spiral.

Rnd 2: (2 sc) 6 times. (12)

Rnd 3: [(2 sc), 1 sc] 6 times. (18)

Rnd 4: [(2 sc), 2 sc] 6 times. (24)

Rnd 5: [(2 sc), 7 sc] 3 times. (27)

Rnds 6 -11: Sc evenly. (27)

Sl st to next st to join.

You'll now work on his broken-wood head accents.

Rnd 12: You'll be crocheting triangular-ish and rectangular-ish shapes, and then slip stitching down one side of each shape to get your hook back to Rnd 11. We do this so we don't have to break off and re join over and over again to continue our work. I broke each shape into different paragraphs so that they are easier to see and organize.

Ch 1, 3 sc evenly. Ch 1, turn. 3 sc evenly. Ch 1, turn. Sk 1 st, 2 sc evenly. Sl st down the side of the rows you just worked until you are about to work into Rnd 11 again.

4 sc evenly. Ch 1, turn. 4 sc evenly. Ch 1, turn. Sk 1 st, 1 sc, sk 1 st, 1 sc. Ch 1, turn. Sk 1 st, 1 sc. Ch 1, turn. Sl st down the side of the rows you just worked until you are about to work into Rnd 11 again.

4 sc evenly. Ch 1, turn. 4 sc evenly. Ch 1, turn. 3 sc, sk last st. Ch 1, turn. 3 sc. Ch 1, turn. Sk 1, 1 sc. Sl st down the side of the rows you just worked until you are about to work into Rnd 11 again.

3 sc evenly. Ch 1, turn. 3 sc evenly. Ch1, turn. 1 sc, sk 1, sl st. Sl st down the side of the rows you just worked until you are about to work into Rnd 11 again.

4 sc evenly. Ch 1, turn. 4 sc evenly. Ch 1, turn. Sk 1 st, 1sc, sk 1 st, 1 sc. Ch 1, turn. Sk 1 st, 1 sc. Ch 1, turn. Sl st down the side of the rows you just worked until you are about to work into Rnd 11 again.

3 sc evenly. Ch 1, turn. 3 sc evenly. Ch1, turn. sk 1, 2 sc. Sl st down the side of the rows you just worked until you are about to work into Rnd 11 again.

3 sc evenly. Ch 1, turn. 1 sc , sk 1, 1 sc. Ch1, turn. Sk 1, 1 sc. Sl st down the side of the rows you just worked until you are about to work into Rnd 11 again.

3 sc evenly. Ch 1, turn. 3 sc evenly. Ch1, turn. 1 sc, sk 1, sl st. Sl st down the side of the rows you just worked until you are about to work into Rnd 11 again.

Sl st into Rnd 11 and break off. Weave in end.

Insert eyes. You get to decide which part of the head should be the face.

Now you'll finish the top of the head. You're just making a circle to cover the hole.

Head Part B

With Brown, repeat Rnds 1-4 of Head Part A.

Sl st to next st to join. Break off leaving 24 inches of yarn.

If you want a branch or two sticking out of his head, crochet these now and sew them to the top of Head Part B before you sew it to the top of Head Part A.

Branch
With Brown and H hook, ch 8, sk 1 ch, work 2 sl st evenly. Ch 4, sk 1 ch, work 3 sl st evenly, then continue to sl st evenly down original ch. Break off.

Short Branch
With Brown and H hook, ch 6, sk 1 ch, work 2 sl st evenly. Ch 3, sk 1 ch, work 2 sl st evenly, then continue to sl st evenly down original ch. Break off.

Lightly stuff Head Part A.

Since Head Part B is 24 sts around and open hole of Head Part A is technically 27 sts around, you can't sew stitch for stitch, so just sew it on as best you can and make it look good. I found that using a 27 st circle was too big for the opening. You can use Rnd 11 of Head Part A as a guide for sewing. While sewing, you also don't want the head to look like it has Frankenstein stitches going all around it, so try to sew as invisibly as you can. Put in more stuffing if needed.

Body

Repeat Rnds 1-4 of Head Part A.

Rnd 5: [(2 sc), 3 sc] 6 times. (30)

Rnds 6-7: Sc evenly. (30)

Rnd 8: [dec, 3 sc] 6 times. (24)

Rnd 9: [dec, 2 sc] 6 times. (18)

Rnd 10: [dec, 4 sc] 3 times. (15)

Put in some stuffing or your sack of poly pellets. If you plan to wire the Body, anchor the bottom wire now if you like, but you can also run the wire after you complete the Body if you don't have a bag of pellets at the bottom.

Rnd 11: [dec, 3 sc] 3 times. (12)

Rnds 12-13: Sc evenly. (12)

Rnd 14: [dec, 2 sc] 3 times. (9)

Rnds 15 – 25: Sc evenly, stuffing lightly as you go. (9) (Note, I worked to 25 rnds because at first I was measuring the Body against a piece of pipe cleaner that I had. You can make him as tall as you like. For a longer Groot, I crocheted until the Body was about 6 inches long.)

Sl st to next st to join. Break off leaving 18 inches of yarn for sewing.

Sew top of Body to bottom of Head Part A. If you are wiring the body, trim the wire so that it reaches about half way into the head, and then poke the wire into the bottom of the head before sewing.

To prepare Arms, fold each end of the pipe cleaner to its center and then twist. If you are using wire, simply measure out the full length that you need for both arms.

Super Heroes Crochet Ideas

Use a pointy stick to stab through top of Body where Arms will go. I go 1 rnd below the the very top of the neck. This will help guide the pipe cleaner arms through the body, but is not necessary for wire. Slide twisted pipe cleaner into place.

You can now determine how long you want the arms and lengthen/shorten the pipe cleaner/wire accordingly. If you are using wire, bend the ends in now so that they are not so pokey.

Arms (make 2)
Pull out about 10 inches of Brown yarn for sewing later.

With H hook, ch 3 and sl st to 1st ch to form ring. (Don't make a magic circle, or if you do, keep the opening loose because you need to fit the pipe cleaner through this hole.)

Rnd 1: Ch 1, work 4 sc into ring. (4)

Rnds 2 – 8: Sc evenly around. (4)

Slip Arm through pipe cleaner to see if it fits. Keep working evenly if you need more coverage.

When you reach the length that you need, create the finger branches.

Sl st to next st to join.

Ch 3, sk 1st ch, sl st 2 times. Sl st to next st.

Ch 5, sk 1 st ch, sl st 4 times. Sl st to next st.

Ch 4, sk 1st ch, sl st 3 times. Sl st to next st.

Sl st to next st. Break off.

While weaving in your end, also sew through the base of the fingers to pull the fingers inward so they are not splayed too open.

Super Heroes Crochet Ideas

Slide Arm back onto pipe cleaner and then sew to body. Repeat on other side.

Leaves

The number of leaves and their placement are up to you!

With Green and F hook, ch 5 or ch 4 and sl st to 1st ch to form your leaf. Break off.

Tie leaf onto tree with yarn tails and then carefully weave in ends and/or hide them inside the tree.

Twisty Body Bits

If you want to add some twisty/viney bits to the body, simply work a length of chains about 12 – 18 inches for a shorter tree and 24 inches for a taller tree with Brown and H hook, then wrap chain lengths around Body, sewing down at each end, and also tacking down with a few stitches around the middle wherever you want to make sure the vine stays put. I only made 2 lengths of chain, but you can add more, or put some on the arms, if you like!

Final Assembly

– Embroider a smile with black yarn or embroidery thread.

– Place baby Groot inside a small pot.

– Fill in with smooth pebbles to keep him upright. You might also need some pebbles underneath, so that he is not sitting too low in the pot.

– Decorate with fake moss.

– If you are giving this as a gift, and you don't want anything to move around, you can also hot glue your baby Groot to the bottom of your pot, or glue something to the bottom of the pot for him to stand on, and then glue him to that, then cover with pebbles, moss, or both!

Spider Man

Materials

Size G hook

Yarn- Red, Blue, Light Blue, Light Yellow, a small amount of Black

Felt- Black, White, Red

Yarn Needle

Glue

Head-red

Rnd 1. Sc 6 in magic ring (6)

Rnd 2. Inc around (12)

Rnd 3. *Inc, Sc in next sc* around (18)

Rnd 4. *Inc, Sc in next 2 sc* around (24)

Rnd 5. *Inc, Sc in next 3 sc* around (30)

Rnd 6. *Inc, Sc in next 4 sc* around (36)

Rnd 7. *Inc, Sc in next 5 sc* around (42)

Rnd 8-15. Sc around

Rnd 16. *Dec, Sc in next 5 sc* around (36)

Rnd 17. *Dec, Sc in next 4 sc* around (30)

Rnd 18. *Dec, Sc in next 3 sc* around (24)

Rnd 19. *Dec, Sc in next 2 sc* around (18)

Rnd 20. *Dec, Sc in next sc* around (12) F/O and Stuff

Body-start with red

The body is worked in closed rounds, not as a spiral.

In the beginning of each round, continue working in the same stitch you slst-ed in.

When counting stitches, the slst doesn't count as a stitch.

Ch 12, slst to close

Rnd 1. Ch 1, *Sc in next sc, Inc* around, slst in next sc (18)

Rnd 2. Ch 1, *Sc in next 2 sc, Inc* around. Switch to blue, slst in next sc (24)

Rnd 3. Ch 1, Sc 7, Sc 10, Sc 7, slst in next sc

Rnd 4. Ch 1, Inc, Sc 6, Inc, Sc 8, Inc, Sc 6, Inc, slst in next sc (28)

Rnd 5. Ch 1, Inc, Sc 9, Inc, Sc 6, Inc, Sc 9, Inc, slst in next sc (32)

Rnd 6-9. Ch 1, Sc 13, Sc 6, Sc 13, slst in next sc

Rnd 10. Ch 1, Hdc around, Switch to blue, slst in next sc

Rnd 11. Ch 1, *Sc in next 6 sc, Dec* around, slst in next sc (28)

Rnd 12. Ch 1, *Sc in next 5 sc, Dec* around, slst in next sc (24)

Rnd 13. Ch 1, *Sc in next 2 sc, Dec* around, slst in next sc (18)

Rnd 14. Ch 1, *Sc in next sc, Dec* around, slst in next sc (12)

Rnd 15. Ch 1, Dec around, slst in next sc (6) F/O, Close, and Stuff

Legs-start with red (make 2)

The arms are worked in closed rounds, not as a spiral.

In the beginning of each round, continue working in the same stitch you slst-ed in.

When counting stitches, the slst doesn't count as a stitch.

Rnd 1. Sc 6 in magic ring, slst in first sc (6)

Rnd 2. Inc around (12)

Rnd 3. *Sc in next 3 sc, Inc* around (15)

Rnd 4. Sc around

Rnd 5. *Sc in next 3 sc, Dec* around (12)

Rnd 6. *Sc in next 2 sc, Dec* around, Switch to blue (9)

Rnd 7. Sc around

Rnd 8. Sc 6, Inc X3 (12) F/O and Stuff

Arms-start with red (make 2)

Rnd 1. Sc 6 in magic ring, slst in next sc (6)

Rnd 2. Ch 1, Inc around, slst in next sc (12)

Rnd 3. Ch 1, Sc around, slst in next sc

Rnd 4. Ch 1, *Sc in next sc, Dec* around, Switch to blue. Slst in next sc (8)

Rnd 5-8. Ch 1, Sc 2, Sc 4, Sc 2, slst in next sc

Switch to red

Rnd 9. Ch 1, Sc around, Slst in next sc

Rnd 10. Ch 1, *Sc in next 2 sc, Dec* around, Slst in next sc (6) F/O and Stuff

Jacket-light yellow

Row 1. Ch 19. Turn

Row 2. Sc in second ch from hook, sc across. Turn (18)

Row 3. Ch 1, Sc 2, Ch 5, Skip 4 sc, Sc 6, Ch 5, Skip 4, Sc 2. Turn (20)

Row 4. Ch 1, Sc 9, Inc X2, Sc 9. Turn(22)

Row 5. Ch 1, Sc 1, (Inc, Sc 2)X2, Inc, Sc 6, Inc, (Sc 2, Inc)X2, Sc 1. Turn (28)

Row 6-7. Ch 1, Sc around. Turn

Row 8. Ch 1, Sc 2, Inc, Sc 22, Inc, Sc 2. Turn (30)

Rnd 9-10. Ch 1, Sc around. Turn

Row 11. Ch 1, Sc 2, Inc, Sc 24, Inc, Sc 2. Turn (32)

Row 12. Ch 1, Sc around. Turn

Sc around edge (only on zipper and collar edge). F/O.

Large Collar-light yellow (make 2)

Row 1. Ch 7. Turn
Row 2. Sc in second ch from hook, sc across. Turn (6)
Row 3. Sc in next 3 sc, Hdc, Dc, Tr. F/O

Sew Large Collar onto Jacket

<u>Small Collar-light yellow</u>
Count however many sc's lie on the Jacket's collar between the two Large Collars. Mine was 18.
Row 1. Ch your number sc's, then add 3. Turn
Row 2. Sc in fourth ch from hook, Dc twice in next ch, sc across until the last, Dc twice in last ch. F/O

Sew Small Collar onto Jacket

<u>Blue Inner Edge-light blue</u>
Row 1. Ch 44, turn (make sure it can run along the inner length of the jacket. Roughly, there should be 12 ch running the length of the zipper edges and 18 ch on the collar edge. Make adjustments if necessary)
Row 2. Hdc in third ch from hook, Hdc across. (42) F/O

Sew Blue Inner Edge to the inside of the Jacket where the edge of it is still slightly visible.

<u>Arms-light yellow (make 2)</u>

The arms are not worked in a spiral, but in rounds.

In the beginning of each round, continue working in the same stitch you slst-ed in.

When counting stitches, the slst doesn't count as a stitch.

Attach yarn to arm hole.

Rnd 1. Ch 1, (Sc 4, Inc twice)X2, slst in next sc (16)

Rnd 2-6. Ch 1, Sc around, slst in next sc F/O

Hoodie-light blue

The hoodie are not worked in a spiral, but in rounds.

In the beginning of each round, continue working in the same stitch you slst-ed in.

When counting stitches, the slst doesn't count as a stitch.

Rnd 1. Hdc 8 in magic ring, slst in next sc (8)

Rnd 2. Ch 1, *Hdc twice in next sc* around, slst in next sc (16)

Rnd 3. Ch 1, *Hdc twice in next sc* around, slst in next sc (32)

Rnd 4. Ch 1, *Hdc in next st, Inc* around, slst in next sc (48)

Rnd 5-9. Ch 1, Hdc around, slst in next sc

Rnd 10. Ch 1, Sc around, slst in next sc. F/O

Make sure Hoodie fits properly and sew the back of it to the Blue Inner Edge

Assembly-

1. Sew Head to Body.

2. Sew Arms (blue side facing towards body) and Legs to Body. To get him to sit properly, I sewed the feet of a little closer to his belly as seen in the pictures.

3. Cut out Eyes from black and white felt and sew/glue on to Head

4. Cut out Spider logo from black and red felt and glue to body. Sew legs with black yarn for black spider logo.

5. Slip on jacket for coolness effect. (The arms can be a bit tough to get through, but just go for it)

Super Heroes Crochet Ideas

The Flash

Materials:

- Worsted weight yarn in red.
- Worsted weight yarn in yellow.
- Worsted weight yarn in skin color.
- Worsted weight yarn in White.
- 9mm Safety Eyes
- Size E (3.5mm) Crochet Hook
- Yarn Needle
- Fiberfil

Instructions:

This pattern is written in American Standard Terms.

Place a marker in the first stitch of every round to indicate the beginning and move the marker up at the start of each new round.

All stitches are worked through both loops unless otherwise indicated.

Instructions between ** are to be repeated until the end of the round.

Instructions between [] are made in the same st.

Numbers between () indicate the total amount of stitches in that round.

When making color changes, remember to always change to the new color before the last yarn over of the last stitch in the old color.

Head:

Worked in the round without joining.

Round 1: With red, 4 sc in MC. (4)

Round 2: 3 sc in each st. (12)

Round 3: sc, *3 sc, sc 2* repeat 3 times, 3 sc, sc. (20)

Round 4: sc 2, *3 sc, sc 4* repeat 3 times, 3 sc, sc 2. (28)

Round 5: sc 3, *3 sc, sc 6* repeat 3 times, 3 sc, sc 3. (36)

Round 6: sc 4, *2 sc, sc 8* repeat 3 times, 2 sc, sc 4. (40)

Round 7-10: sc around. (40)

Round 11: With red, sc 19. Change to skin color, 2 sc in next 2 sts. Change to red, sc 19. (42)

Round 12: With red, sc 15. Change to skin color, sc. Change to red, sc 2. Change to skin color, sc 2, sk next 2 sts, sc 2. *(This creates the nose.)* Change to red, sc 2. Change to skin color, sc. Change to red, sc 15. (40)

Round 13-15: With red, sc 15. Change to skin color, sc 10. Change to red, sc 15. (40)

Round 16: With red, sc around. (40)

Place 9mm eyes between rounds 11-12 spacing 4 sts apart. Each eye should be in the center of each red area on either side of the nose.

Round 17: sc 3, *dec twice, sc 6* repeat 3 times, dec twice, sc 3. (32)

Round 18: sc 2, *dec twice, sc 4* repeat 3 times, dec twice. sc 2. (24)

Begin Stuffing head.

Round 19: sc, *dec twice, sc 2* repeat 3 times, dec twice, sc. (16)

Round 20: *dec* around. (8)

Finish stuffing. Sew opening closed and leave long tail for sewing head to body.

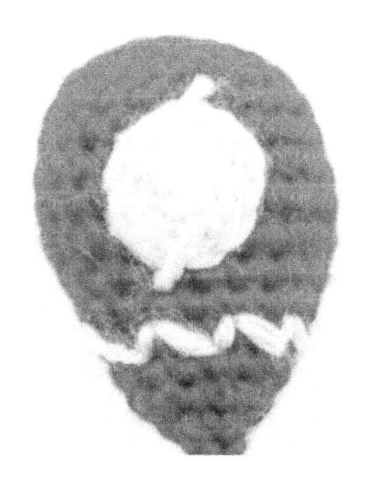

Body:

Worked in the round without joining.

Round 1: With red, 6 sc in MC. (6)

Round 2: Inc in each st around. (12)

Round 3: *sc, inc* repeat around. (18)

Round 4: *sc 2, inc* repeat around. (24)

Round 5-9: sc around. (24)

Round 10: *6 sc, sc dec 3 times* repeat twice. (18)

Round 11: sc around. (18)

Round 12: *5 sc, sc dec twice* repeat twice. (14)

Round 13: sc around. (14)

Begin stuffing.

Round 14: *3 sc, sc dec twice* repeat twice. (10)

Round 15: *sc dec* around. (5)

Finish stuffing and sew seam closed. Leave long tail for sewing head to body. Pull yarn through middle of body. Sew head to body.

Body Stitching: With yellow and threaded through the needle, insert the needle 3 rounds up from the bottom of the body and *make a diagonal line [3 sts to the left and up one st], make a straight line down one st below.* Repeat pattern between ** around the body.

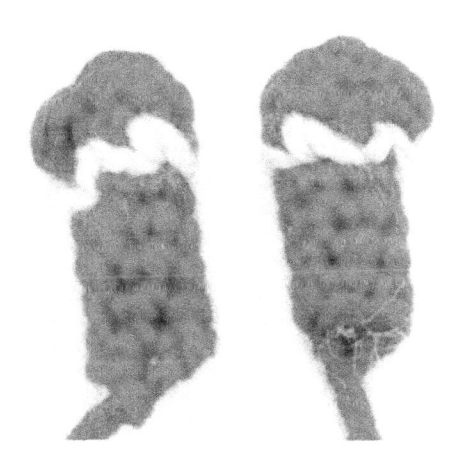

Arms (2):

Worked in the round without joining.

Round 1: With red, 6 sc in MC. (6)

Round 2: sc, inc, work thumb [ch 1, sc in previous sc made, sl st in the same sp as inc], *sc,inc* twice. (8)

Round 3: *sc, dec* repeat around. *Keep thumb in front of stitches.* (6)

Round 4-8: sc around. (6)

Lightly Stuff. Leave long tail for sewing onto Body.

Arm Stitching: Insert the needle between rounds 3-4 of arm and *make a diagonal line [2 sts to the left and up one st], make a straight line down one st below.* Repeat pattern between ** around the arm above the fist.

Legs (2):
Worked in the round without joining.
Work one left and one right.
Round 1: With yellow, 6 sc in MC. (6)
Round 2: Inc in each st around. (12)
Round 3: *sc, inc* repeat around. (18)

Round 4: In BLO, sc around. (18)

Left Foot

Round 5: sc 10, dec 3 times, sc 2 (15)

Round 6: sc 8, dec 3 times, sc (12)

Right Foot

Round 5: sc 2, dec 3 times, sc 10 (15)

Round 6: sc, dec 3 times, sc 8 (12)

Round 7: sc around. (12)

Round 8: Change to red. In BLO, *sc 2, dec* repeat around. (9)

Round 9: sc around. (9)

Begin Stuffing.

Round 10-12: sl st 3, sc, hdc 4, sc. (9)

Finish stuffing. Leave long tail for sewing onto Body.

Emblem:

Worked in the round without joining.

Round 1: With white, sc 4 in MC. (4)

Round 2: Inc in each st around. (8)

FO. Leave long tail for sewing.

With yellow, join to the emblem and sl st in each st around. FO.

FO. Weave in ends.

Sew emblem to body between rounds 6-9. With yellow, stitch a thunderbolt on top of emblem and body.

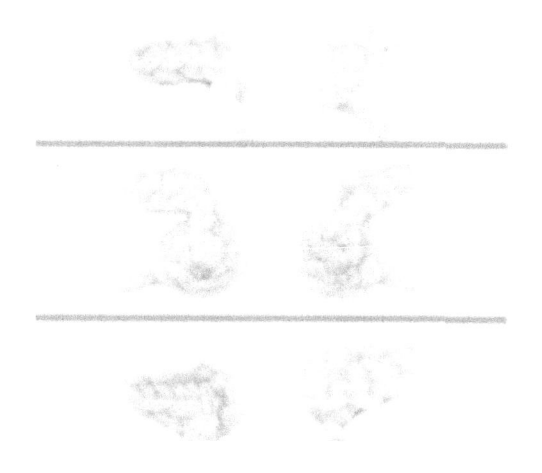

Helmet Wings:
Worked in the round without joining.
Round 1: With yellow, sc 4 in MC. (4)
Round 2 *sc, inc* repeat around. (6)
FO. Leave long tail for sewing.
With yellow, ch 8. sc in 2nd ch from hook and next 2 chs, sk 2 chs, sl st in last 2 chs.

FO. Leave long tail for sewing to circle previously made. Sew Helmet wings to the sides of the head between rounds 10-13, 4 sts from the face.

Boot Wings:

With yellow, ch 6. sc in 2nd ch from hook and next ch, sk 2 chs, sl in last ch.

FO. Leave long tail for sewing to boots.

Super Heroes Crochet Ideas

Doctor Strange

Materials:

– Cream, navy, blue, red, black and white yarn (I used 100% cotton yarn **Barroco** by Círculo, which is a bulky / 12 ply (7wpi));
– Thin black yarn to embroider (I used 100% cotton yarn **Anne** by Círculo, which is a Fingering / 4 ply (14 wpi));
– Thin brown and silver yarn (I used 100% cotton yarn **Anne** by Círculo, which is a Fingering / 4 ply (14 wpi) and thin gold yarn (I used 100% cotton yarn Esterlina 5 by Círculo, which has a metalic look and is a Light Fingering);
– 4mm and 2mm crochet hook;
– Fiberfill;
– Tapestry needle, needle and scissors;
– Safety eyes 13mm;
– Pins.

Notes:

– I always do my crochet works using continuous rounds. I will let you know when you have to join rounds;

– Everytime I will do a crochet work, the first thing I do is take a look in the entirely pattern before start doing it, so, I can have an idea of how the pattern works. Well, I recommend you to do the same;

– For sewing the pieces together you will use the tapestry needle;

Recently, I'm having a hard time to answer all the questions sent to my email and the comments. I'm sorry that I'm not able to answer your doubts. However, if you have any doubt, I'm sure that it is worth to leave a comment here, because even if I can't answer you, I'm sure that someone in the community will try to help you out ^^

Pattern:

Head:

R1: 6 sc in MC (6)

R2: inc (12)

R3: sc, inc (18)

R4: 2 sc, inc (18)

R5: 3 sc, inc (30)

R6-13: sc in each sc (30)

R14: 3 sc, dec (24)

R15: 2 sc, dec (18)

Place the safety eyes between Rounds 10 and 11. Leave about 5 holes between the eyes.

R16: sc, dec (12)

Bordar a barba

R17: sc, dec (9)

Finish off and leave a long tail for sewing.

Ears:

R1: Ch 4, 3 sc from the second ch from hook (3)

Finish off and leave a long tail for sewing.

Hair:

R1: 6 sc in MC (6)

R2: inc (12)

R3: sc, inc (18)

R4: 2 sc, inc (24)

R5: 3 sc, inc (30)

R6: sc in each sc (30)

R7: Make a sl st in the next stitch, then make 2 ch and a dc in the same stitch. After that make 16 dc (17)

R8: ch2, turn, 17 dc (17)

R9: ch2, turn, dec, 13 dc, dec (15)

R10: ch2, turn, dec, 11 dc, dec (13)

R11: ch2, turn, dec, 9 dc, dec (11)

Finish off.

Now we are going to do his chops (the hair near his ears and ahead them). For that, attach the black yarn in the stitch next to the 1st dc and make one dc in this stitch. Then, ch1, turn and make another dc. Finish off. One is done, now make the same thing on the other side. (Watch the video to have a better idea)

"Bangs":

Right strand: ch 6, then, with a tapestry needle, hide the yarn in the back part of the chain until it reachs the 1st ch. Cut the yarn and leave a piece to sew it to his head.

Middle strand: ch 5, then, with a tapestry needle, hide the yarn in the back part of the chain until it reachs the 1st ch. Cut the yarn and leave a piece to sew it to his head.

Left strand: ch 5, then, with a tapestry needle, hide the yarn in the back part of the chain until it reachs the 1st ch. Cut the yarn and leave a piece to sew it to his head.

Body and legs (work joining rounds):

Start with blue yarn

R1: ch 5, 2 sc in 2nd chain from hook, 2 sc, 3 sc in the last chain, 2 sc, sc (10)

R2: 2 inc, 2 sc, 3 inc, 2 sc, inc (16)

R3-R7: sc in each sc (16)

Change to navy

R8: make one sc in each sc, using only back loops (16)

R9: 6 sc, sc in the 15th sc, sc in the 16th sc (8)

R10: sc in each sc (8)

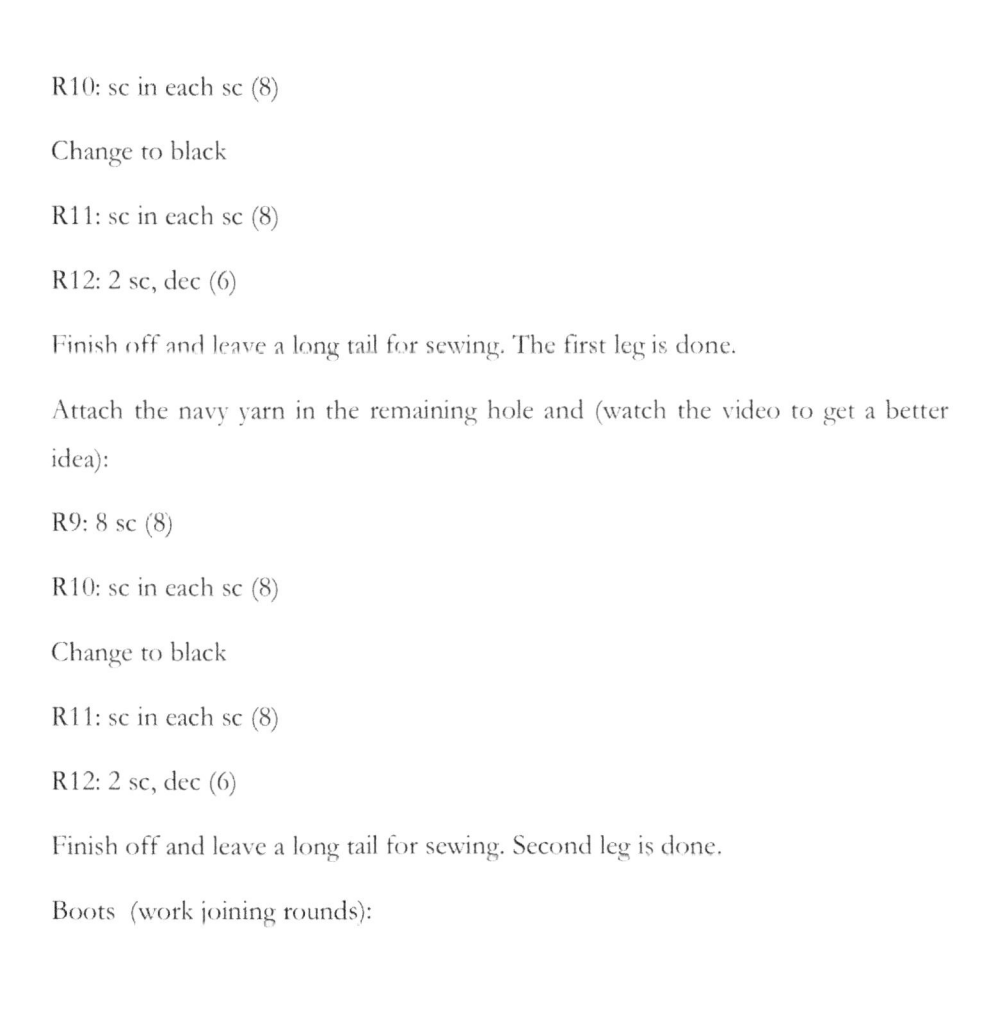

Change to black

R11: sc in each sc (8)

R12: 2 sc, dec (6)

Finish off and leave a long tail for sewing. The first leg is done.

Attach the navy yarn in the remaining hole and (watch the video to get a better idea):

R9: 8 sc (8)

R10: sc in each sc (8)

Change to black

R11: sc in each sc (8)

R12: 2 sc, dec (6)

Finish off and leave a long tail for sewing. Second leg is done.

Boots (work joining rounds):

R1: ch 6, inc in the 2nd ch from hook, 3 sc, 3 sc in the last chain, 3 sc, sc in the last chain (12)

R2: 4 sc, 3 dec, 2 sc(9)

R3: 2 sc, 3 dec, sc (6)

Finish off.

Bottom of his tunic:

R1: ch 17, sc 16 (16)

R2: ch 2, turn, dc on dec, hdc, 10 sc, hdc, dc on dec (14)

Finish off and leave a long tail for sewing.

Belt:

Use a thinner brown yarn and 2mm hook.

R1: Ch 121, sc 120 (120)

Finish off.

Silver ring (Use a thinner silver yarn and 2mm hook):

R1: 10 sc in MC, leave a small hole to pass the belt through it (10)

Finish off.

Arms:

Start with navy

R1: ch 5, sc 4 (4)

R2: ch 2, attach the yarn in the 1st stitch in order to make a circle and then make 6 sc (6)

R3-5: sc (6)

Change to blue

R6: sc (6)

R7: sc just in the front loops (6)

Change to cream

R8: sc (6)

R9: 2 sc, inc (8)

R10: 2 sc, dec (6)

Finish off.

Eye of Agamotto (Use a thinner gold yarn and 2mm hook):

R1: 6 sc in MC (6)

R2: hdc, dc, hdc, hdc, dc, hdc (6)

finish off.

necklace (use a thinner brown yarn and 2mm hook):

R1: 30 ch (3)

Finish off.

Clock of Levitation:

Top:

R1: ch 16, dc 14 (14)

R2: inc, dc 12, inc (16)

R3: inc, dc 14, inc (18)

Finish off.

Attach the yarn to the back of the first chain and make this:

Bottom:

R1: inc, dc 12, inc (16)

R2: dec, dc 12, dec (14)

R3: dec, dc 10, dec (12)

R4-6: dc in each dc (12)

Finish off.

Assembly:

1. Make his head until round 15:

Then place the safety eyes between rounds 11-12 and make Round 16.

After that embroider his eyebrows and beard using a thinner yarn. You may use some pins to mark where you should embroid. (In my video you can have an idea of what I did).

Super Heroes Crochet Ideas

2. Sew his ears to his head. Top of the ear should be sewn between rounds 9 and 10.

3. Sew his hair to his head.

3.1. First sew the bottom part of his hair (the one near his neck)

3.2. Keep going and sew the part near his ear (it's on the back of his ear):

3.3 Then, sew his chop:

3.4. And sew his chop to the part of his hair that you have already sewn behind his ear (you have to do this in order to hide the cream part) (It's better to watch the video to get a clear idea):

3.5. Then, sew the front part of his hair and keep going until the end.

4. Sew the white lines into his head

5. Sew his "bangs" to his hair. First sew the "right strand" in the middle of his head. Then sew the "middle strand" next to it and finally the "left strand" next to the last one.

6. Make his body and boots and sew them together;

7. Sew the bottom of his tunic to his body. Use the loops left in Round 8 of the body to sew the tunic to the body. Leave an empity space in the center as shown in the photo.

Super Heroes Crochet Ideas

8. Make his belt and silver ring and place it his his body. Attach lightly the silver ring to his body with a few stitches.

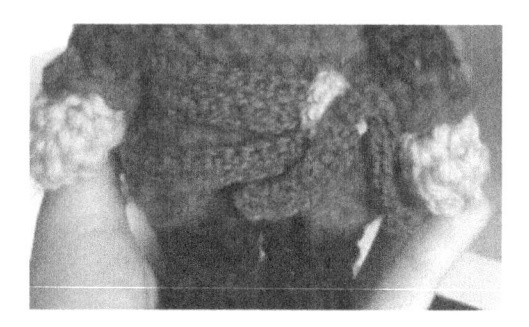

9. Sew his head to his body. I needed to put an wire inside his head and body, because his head was too heavy and it wasn't sustaining;

Super Heroes Crochet Ideas

10. Make his arms and sew to his body;

11. Sew the clock of levitation to his body

12. Sew the eye of Agamotto to his neck.

Batman and Robin

Materials

Worsted weight yarn: Black, Dark gray, Skin color, Yellow

White, black, yellow felt

Black and yellow embroidery floss

Embroidery needle

Stuffing

F hook, G hook

Yarn needle

Tacky glue

Head

Skin color and F hook

R1: sc 6 in magic ring

R2: inc around (12st)

R3: *sc 1, inc* around (18 st)

R4: *sc 2, inc* around (24)

R5: *sc 3, inc* around (30)

R6: *sc 4, inc* around (36 St)

R7-13: sc in each st around (36)

R14: *sc 4, dec* around (30)

R15: *sc 3, dec* around (24)

R16: *sc 2, dec* around (18st)

FO with long tail for sewing

Cowl

Start with black yarn and a larger Hook (eg, G)

R1: sc 6 in magic ring

R2: inc around (12st)

R3: *sc 1, inc* around (18 st)

R4: *sc 2, inc* around (24)

R5: *sc 3, inc* around (30)

R6: *sc 4, inc* around (36 St)

R7-12: sc in each st around (36)

R13: sc in 28 St, leave last 8 st

R14: ch1, turn, *sc in 4 St, dec* around until last St, then 2 sc in last St

R15: ch1, turn, 2sc in first St, *sc in 4st, dec* around, then 2 sc in last St

R16: ch1, turn, 2 sc in first St, *sc in 3st, dec* around, then 2 sc in last St, chain 4, fo with long tail

Body

Start with black and F hook

R1: sc 6 in magic ring

R2: 2sc in each st around (12st)

R3: *sc, inc* repeat around (18st)

R4: *sc 2, inc* repeat around (24st)

R5: *sc 3, inc* repeat around (30st)

R6: sc around (30st)

switch to gray

R7-9: sc around (30st)

R10: *sc 3, dec* repeat around (24st)

R11-13: sc around (24st)

R14: *sc 2, dec* repeat around (18st)

FO with long tail for sewing, stuff

Arms (make two)

Start with black yarn and F hook

R1: sc 6 in magic ring

R2: *sc 2, inc* repeat around (8st)

Switch to dark gray yarn

R3-7: sc around (8st)

R8: dec around (4st), fo with long tail for sewing – don't stuff

Feet (make two)

Start with black yarn and F hook

R1: sc 5 in magic ring

R2: inc around (10st)

Switch to gray yarn

R3-5: sc around (10st)

Fo with long tail for sewing, stuff

Ears (make two)

Black yarn on F hook

R1: sc 3 in magic ring

R2: inc around (6st)

R3: *sc 1, inc* around (9 St)

Fo with long tail for sewing. Flatten.

Belt

Yellow yarn, F hook

CH 31, fo with long tail

Batman's pieces

Assembly

It's easier to deal with the head and body separately, then attach them together as the final step.

Head: Tuck head inside cowl and tie the strap around his chin. Sew black ears parallel on either side of his head. Embroider mouth with black floss. Cut two white triangles and glue on for eye holes.

Body: Sew legs and arms onto body. Tie belt around waist where the yarn color changes. You may want to secure the belt with a few stitches or glue. Cut one large piece of black felt for the cape and sew onto shoulders with black floss. Cut bat symbol out of black felt, glue onto a circle of yellow felt, and glue onto the middle of chest.

When all of the glue is dried on both pieces, sew head onto body.

Robin the Boy Wonder

Materials

Worsted weight yarn: Black, Green, Yellow, Red, Skin color

Yellow, black, white felt

Black and yellow embroidery floss

Embroidery needle

Yarn needle

Stuffing

F hook

Tacky glue

Head

Skin color and F hook

R1: sc 6 in magic ring

R2: inc around (12st)

R3: *sc 1, inc* around (18 st)

R4: *sc 2, inc* around (24)

R5: *sc 3, inc* around (30)

R6: *sc 4, inc* around (36 St)

R7-13: sc in each st around (36)

R14: *sc 4, dec* around (30)

R15: *sc 3, dec* around (24)

R16: *sc 2, dec* around (18st)

FO with long tail for sewing

Hair (optional, see assembly notes)

Black yarn

R1: sc 6 in magic ring

R2: inc around (12st)

R3: *sc 1, inc* around (18 st)

R4: *sc 2, inc* around (24)

R5: *sc 3, inc* around (30)

R6: *sc 4, inc* around (36 St)

R7: sc around (36)

FO with long tail for sewing

Body

Start with green

R1: sc 6 in magic ring

R2: inc around (12st)

R3: *sc, inc* repeat around (18st)

R4: *sc 2, inc* repeat around (24st)

Switch to red

R5-9: sc around (24st)

R10: *sc 3, dec* repeat around (18st)

R11-14: sc around (18st)

Fo, stuff

Arms (make two)

Start with green yarn

R1: sc 6 in magic ring

R2: *sc 2, inc* repeat around (8st)

R3: sc around (8st)

switch to skin color

R4-6: sc around (8st)

switch to green

R7: sc around (8st)

R8: dec around (4st), fo with long tail for sewing – don't stuff

Feet (make two)

Start with green yarn

R1: sc 5 in magic ring

R2: inc around (10st)

Switch to skin color

R3-4: sc around (10st)

Switch to green

R5: sc around (10)

Fo with long tail for sewing, stuff

Belt

Yellow yarn, F hook

CH 25, fo with long tail

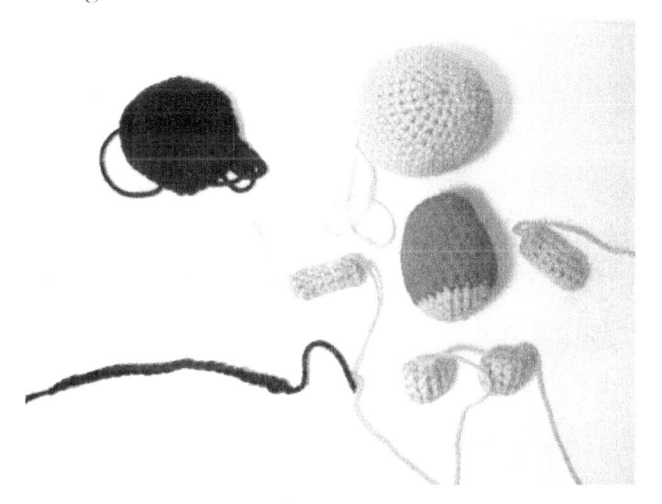

Robin's pieces

Assembly

It's easier to deal with the head and body separately, then attach them together as the final step.

Head: To make Robin's hair, there are different options. The easiest method is to fasten on strands of black yarn all over the scalp, but this leaves a rather shaggy hairstyle. For a smoother hairstyle, make a black disk (see above) and sew on top of the head. Embroider bangs on the front with black yarn. Go down the back with two rows of double crochets.

Embroider mouth with black floss: to make a smile, curve thread and secure with a pin, then glue in place. Cut black mask and two white circles out of felt and glue on for mask and eyes.

Body: Sew legs and arms onto body. Tie belt around waist above where the yarn color changes. You may want to secure the belt with a few stitches or glue. You can also add a belt buckle with a small circle of yellow felt. Cut one large piece of yellow felt for the cape and sew onto shoulders with yellow floss. Cut a small black circle and attach to the upper left chest with the letter R in yellow floss.

When all of the glue is dried on both pieces, sew head onto body.

Wonder Woman

Materials:

– Worsted weight yarn in red.

– Worsted weight yarn in blue.

– Worsted weight yarn in skin color.

– Worsted weight yarn in yellow.

– Worsted weight yarn in black.

– Worsted weight yarn in gold.

– Worsted weight yarn in white.

– 9mm Safety Eyes

– Size E (3.5mm) Crochet Hook

– Yarn Needle

– Fiberfil

– Embroidery thread in white and red.

Instructions:

This pattern is written in American Standard Terms.

Place a marker in the first stitch of every round to indicate the beginning and move the marker up at the start of each new round.

All stitches are worked through both loops unless otherwise indicated.

Instructions between ** are to be repeated until the end of the round.

Instructions between [] are made in the same st.

Numbers between () indicate the total amount of stitches in that round.

When making color changes, remember to always change to the new color before the last yarn over of the last stitch in the old color.

Head:

Worked in the round without joining.

Round 1: With skin, 4 sc in MC. (4)

Round 2: 3 sc in each st. (12)

Round 3. sc, *3 sc, sc 2* repeat 3 times, 3 sc, sc. (20)

Round 4: sc 2, *3 sc, sc 4* repeat 3 times, 3 sc, sc 2. (28)

Round 5: sc 3, *3 sc, sc 6* repeat 3 times, 3 sc, sc 3. (36)

Round 6: sc 4, *2 sc, sc 8* repeat 3 times, 2 sc, sc 4. (40)

Round 7-10: sc around. (40)

Round 11: sc 19, 2 sc in next 2 sts, sc 19. (42)

Round 12: sc 20, 2 sc in next 2 sts, sc 20. (44)

Round 13: sc 20, sk 4 sts, sc 20. (40)

Round 14-16: sc around. (40)

Place 9mm eyes between rounds 11-12 spacing 6 sts apart. Each eye should be on either side of the nose.

Round 17: sc 3, *dec twice, sc 6* repeat 3 times, dec twice, sc 3. (32)

Round 18: sc 2, *dec twice, sc 4* repeat 3 times, dec twice. sc 2. (24)

Begin Stuffing head.

Round 19: sc, *dec twice, sc 2* repeat 3 times, dec twice, sc. (16)

Round 20: *dec* around. (8)

Finish stuffing. Sew opening closed and leave long tail for sewing head to the body.

Body:

Worked in the round without joining.

Round 1: With skin, 6 sc in MC. (6)

Round 2: Inc in each st around. (12)

Round 3: *Inc, sc* around. (18)

Round 4: *inc, sc 2* around. (24)

Round 5: With yellow, sc 2. With skin color, sc 8. With yellow, sc 6. With skin color, sc 1. With yellow, sc 1. With skin color, sc 1. With yellow, sc 5. (24)

Round 6: With yellow, sc 4. With skin color, sc 4. With yellow, sc 16. (24)

Round 7: With red, sc 3. With yellow, sc 6. With red, sc 8. With yellow, sc 1. With red, sc 1. With yellow, sc 1. With red, sc 4.

Round 8-9: With red, sc around. (24)

Round 10: With red, dec twice, 6 sc, dec 3 times, sc 3. With yellow, sc 1. With red, sc 2, dec. (18)

Round 11: With yellow, sc around. (18)

Round 12: With blue, *dec twice, sc 5* twice. (14)

Round 13: sc around. (14)

Begin stuffing.

Round 14: *dec twice, sc 3* repeat twice. (10)

Round 15: *sc dec* around. (5)

Finish stuffing and sew seam closed. Pull yarn through middle of body. Sew head to body. With white embroider thread, embroider several stars in random spots on blue part of body.

Arms (2):

Worked in the round without joining.

Round 1: With skin color, 6 sc in MC. (6)

Round 2: sc, inc, work thumb [ch 1, sc in previous sc made, sl st in the same sp as inc], *sc, inc* twice. (9)

Round 3: *sc, dec* around. *Keep thumb in front of stitches.* (6)

Round 4-5: With gold, sc around. (6)

Round 6-8: With skin color, sc around. (6)

Lightly Stuff. Leave long tail for sewing onto Body.

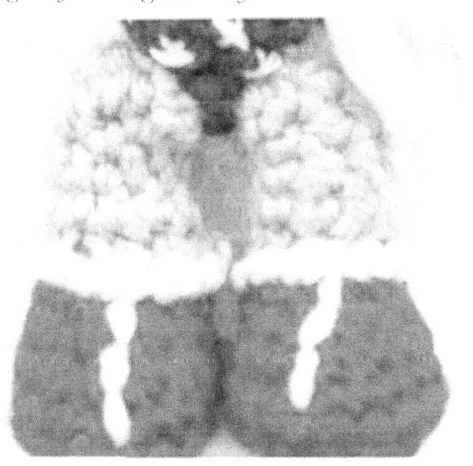

Legs (2):

Worked in the round without joining.

Work one left and one right.

Round 1: With red, 6 sc in MC. (6)

Round 2: Inc in each st around. (12)

Round 3: *sc, inc* around. (18)

Round 4: In BLO, sc around. (18)

Left Foot

Round 5: sc 10, dec 3 times, sc 2 (15)

Round 6: sc 8, dec 3 times, sc (12)

Right Foot

Round 5: sc 2, dec 3 times, sc 10 (15)

Round 6: sc, dec 3 times, sc 8 (12)

Round 7: sc around. (12)

Round 8: Change to skin color. In BLO, *sc 2, dec* around. (9)

Round 9: sc around. (9)

Begin Stuffing.

Round 10-12: sl st 3, sc, hdc 4, sc. (9)

Finish stuffing. Leave long tail for sewing onto Body. With white embroidery thread or white worsted weight yarn, embroider stitching on boots.

Crown:

Worked as one row.

With yellow, ch 23, sc in 2nd ch from hook and next 5 chs, hdc in next 2 chs, dc in next 2 chs, tr in next ch, ch 2, sl st in 2nd ch from hook, tr in next ch, dc in next 2 chs, hdc in next 2 chs, sc in last 6 chs. (22)

Leave long tail for sewing. With red embroidery thread, embroider a star on the front, top of the crown. Sew crown to front of head.

Lasso of Truth:

Wrap yellow yarn around two of your fingers 3-4 times. Sew to side of hip on body.

Hair:

With black yarn, cut 80-90 of approx. 9" strands of yarn. Latch hook hair to top of head.

Super Heroes Crochet Ideas

Loki

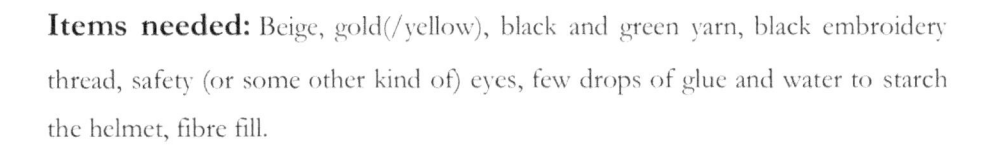

Items needed: Beige, gold(/yellow), black and green yarn, black embroidery thread, safety (or some other kind of) eyes, few drops of glue and water to starch the helmet, fibre fill.

I used 2.0 mm crochet hook and nearly lace weight yarn.

Abbreviations :

MR=Magic Ring

Ch = Chain

St=stitch

Sc = Single crochet

Sl= slip stitch

BLO = Back loops only

INVDEC = Invisible Decrease

INC= Increase

HDC= Half double crochet

Head (beige)

MR 5

1. INC x5 (10 total)

2. INC x10 (20 total)

3. (1 sc next 3 stitches, INC) around (25 total)

4. (1 sc next 4 stitches, INC) around (30 total)

5. (1 sc next 5 stitches, INC around (35 total)

6. (1 sc next 6 stitches, INC) around (40 total)

7-10. Sc around. (40 total st per row for 4 rows)

11. (1sc next 6 stitches, INVDEC) x5 (35 total)

12. (1sc next 5 stitches, INVDEC) x5 (30 total)

13. (1sc next 4 stitches, INVDEC) x5 (25 total)

14. (1sc next 3 stitches, INVDEC) x5 (20 total)

15. Fasten off, leaving a long tail for stitching the head to the body.

(If you are using safety eyes, attach them now.)

Stuff head.

Body (black)

MR 5

1. INC x5 (10 total)

2. INC x10 (20 total)

3. (1 sc next 3 st, INC) around (25 total)

4-7. Sc around (25 total per row for 4 rows)

8. (1 sc next 3 st, INVDEC) x5 (20 total)

9-10. Sc around (20 total per row for 2 rows)

11. (1 sc next 2 st, INVDEC) x5 (15 total)

12. Fasten off.

Stuff body and stitch the head on place.

Leg (make 2) (black)

MR 5

1. INC x5 (10 total)

2. (1 sc next stitch, INC) x5 (15 total)

3. Working in BLO, sc around (15 total)

4-5. Sc around (15 total stitches for 2 rows)

6. (1 sc, INVDEC) x5 (10 total)

7-8. Sc around (10 total stitches for 2 rows)

9. Fasten off, leaving long tail for attaching the leg to the body

Stuff the legs half full, attach to the body.

Arm (make 2) (beige, black and green)

MR 5 with beige yarn.

1. INC x4 (8 total)

2. BLO – sc around (8 total)

continue with black yarn.

3-6. Sc around (8 total st for four rows)

4. Fasten off, leave a long tail for stitching the arm to the body.

Stitch green decorations around the "wrist".

Stitch to the body

chain/necklace/whatever (gold/yellow)

Ch 7 (or as long as you need for suitable length), fasten off and stitch to the body.

Coat (black and green)

with black yarn:

1. Chain 12, turn

2. Sc 11, ch 1, turn

3. Sc 5, ch 1, turn

4. Sc 5, ch 1, turn

5. Sc 5, ch 7, turn

6. Sc 11, ch 1, turn

7-9. repeat row 6

10. Sc 6, ch 6, turn

11. Sc 11, ch 1, turn

12-14. Repeat row 11

15. Sc 5, ch 1, turn

16. Sc 5, ch 1, turn

17. Sc 5, ch 7, turn

18. Sc 11, fasten off

with green yarn:

Sc along the hem, sl up the lapels. The coat should now look like this:

Attach to the body with few stitches near the neck.

Make and attach hair. I used black embroidery floss to get that sleek look, but it is not the easiest yarn to work with and I actually had to use a bit of hair spray (!) to fix the hair. If you don't know how to make and attach hair, this tutorial is really great.

Helmet (gold/yellow)

The helmet isn't entirely symmetrical, but for my purposes it didn't matter. If you are a perfectionist, you might want to work the helmet in joined rounds and not in spiral like I did, and fix the asymmetrical cheek plates.

MR 5

1. INC x5 (10 total)

2. INC x10 (20 total)

3. (1 sc next 3 stitches, INC) around (25 total)

4. (1 sc next 4 stitches, INC) around (30 total)

5. (1 sc next 5 stitches, INC) around (35 total)

6. (1 sc next 6 stitches, INC) around (40 total)

7. (1 sc next 7 stitches, INC) around (45 total)

8. Sc around (45)

9. Sc 27, ch 1, turn

10-12. repeat row 9

13. (start of the first cheek plate) Sc 27, ch 6, turn

14. Sc 15, sl, turn

15. Skip sl and sl in first sc, sc in next 14, ch 1, turn

16. Sc 13, sl, fasten off

(second cheek plate)

1. Sl in 11th st from the "empty" side of the helmet, sc 10 (until the edge), ch 6, turn

2. Sc 13, sl

3. Skip sl, sl in the first sc, sc 12, ch 1

4. Sc 11, sl, fasten off.

Sl around the edge of the whole helmet.

Horns (make 4)

1. Ch 26, turn

2. Sl 14, sc 5, HDC 5

fasten off, leave a long tail

Stitch two horns neatly together (right sides facing out), block to create the curve. Stitch the blocked horns to the helmet.

Depending on how tightly you crochet and what kind of yarn you use, it might be a good idea to starch the helmet, especially the horns. I used solution *1 part glue: 5 parts warm water* to harden and block the helmet.

The staff in some pictures is just an ice cream stick cut to shape. Take an ice cream stick (or something similar), draw the outline on it, cut the excess with a knife (or if you have more sophisticated tools use them), paint it gold and glue a blue bead to it. :) In the pictures it's not actually attached to Loki's hand, just wedged between his hand and foot, but a piece of thin wire should provide a more permanent solution.

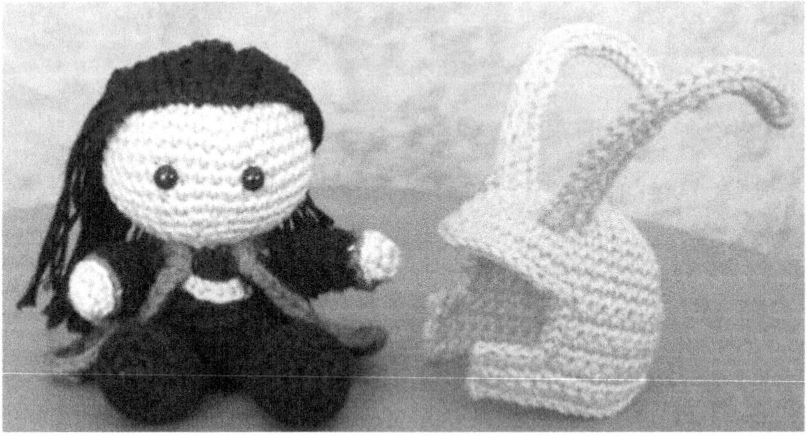

Deadpool

Materials

- red, black, white yarn
- E (3.5mm) crochet hook
- fiberfill
- scissors
- yarn needle

Products from Amazon.com

Notes

- The whole body is worked seamlessly from the bottom up.
- When it says, 'change to [color]' you'll make the color change in the last sc that you make before it says to change color. Meaning you will pick up the new color in the last yarn over of that sc.
- Dc-inc means you will increase with double crochet stitches
- Worked in continuous rounds unless otherwise stated
- All terms in U.S.
- Stitch counts in ( ) at the end of row

Abbreviations

- sc = single crochet
- inc = increase
- dec = invisible decrease
- sl st = slip stitch
- ch = chain

Super Heroes Crochet Ideas

- FLO = front loops only
- BLO = back loops only
- FO = fasten off

Super Heroes Crochet Ideas

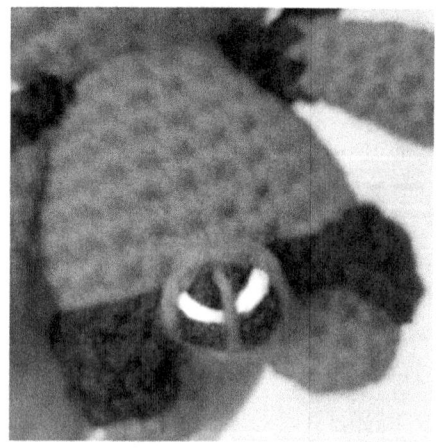

Super Heroes Crochet Ideas

Legs (in red):

1. Sc 6 in a magic ring (6)
2. Inc 6 times (12)
3. Sc around (12)
4. FO first leg.
5. Repeat rounds 1-3, but do not FO and continue below.

Body:

6. Ch 1, join with sl st to first leg at 6th stitch.

7. Sc 11 around first leg.
8. Sc in the chain you made before connecting the two legs.
9. Sl st in the last stitch of 2nd leg to join.
10. Sc 12 around 2nd leg.
11. Sc in the other side of the chain.
12. There will be a total of (26) around (do not count the first sl st).
13. Skipping the first sl st, sc around (26)
14. Sc around (26)
15. Sc around (26)
16. Sc around (26)
17. Sc around (26)
18. Sc around (26)
19. Sc 5, dec, sc 12, dec, sc 5 (24)
20. Sc 5, dec, sc 10, dec, sc 5 (22)
21. Sc 4, dec, sc 10, dec, sc 4 (20)
22. Sc 4, dec, sc 8, dec, sc 4 (18)
23. Start to add stuffing.

24. [Sc, dec] 6 times (12)

25.

Head:

26. FLO: inc in every stitch around (24)

27. [Sc 3, inc] 6 times (30)

28. [Sc 4, inc] 6 times (36)

29. Sc around (36)

30. Sc around (36)

31. Sc around (36)

32. Sc around (36)

33. Sc around (36)

34. Sc around (36)

35. Sc around (36)

36. Sc around (36)

37. [Sc 4, dec] 6 times (30)

38. [Sc 3, dec] 6 times (24)

39. [Sc 2, dec] 6 times (18)

40. Add more stuffing.

41. [Sc, dec] 6 times (12)

42. [Sc 2, dec] 3 times (9)

43. [Sc, dec] 3 times (6)

44. Dec, sc 4 (5)

45. Dec, sc 3 (4)

46. FO, run the tail through the front loops of the last 4 stitches, fold over, and attach the end to the head.

Arms – make 2 (in red):

1. Sc 6 in a magic ring (6)
2. Inc around (12)
3. Sc around (12)

4. [Sc 2, dec] 3 times (9)
5. Sc around (9)
6. Sc around (9)
7. [Sc, dec] 3 times, change to black (6)
8. Sc around (6)
9. Sc around (6)
10. FO & leave a long tail for sewing. You can stuff the arms if you wish, I like to just use the yarn tails and leave them a little flat. Attach at round 15, where the head meets the body.

Belt (in black):

Ch 30, turn & work back on one side of the chains.

Sl st 3, *ch 3, sc 2 back down that chain, ch 1 & turn, sc 2, ch 1 & turn, sc 2, skip 2 on original chain, sl st in next* (this makes the belt pocket), sl st 17, repeat between **, sl st 3. FO and leave a long tail for sewing. Attach at round 6 of the body with the pockets on the front of the legs. I sew the 2 ends together at the front and a few stitches along the belt so it stays in place.

Katanas (in black):

Ch 18, turn and work on one side of the chains.

Sl st 11, ch 12, turn & work back down those chains, sl st 11.

Sl st 1 in the original chain.

Ch 6, turn & work back down those chains, sl st 5.

Sl st 5 in the original chain.

You should have an 'X' with 2 slightly longer sides, those are the tops of the swords.

FO & leave a tail for sewing. Attach at the back of the body.

The next part for the eyes and the belt buckle can be a bit tricky to get the right look, you can always use felt instead if you want those super clean lines.

Super Heroes Crochet Ideas

Felt details

Left eye (in white):

1. Sc 6 in a magic ring (6)

2. Inc x 2, sc 4, change to black (8)
3. In BLO, inc, sc, inc, dc-inc x 2, sc 3 (12)
4. Sc, hdc-inc, sc. FO with a long tail.
5. *Pro tip: use part of the sewing tail to make the color changes neater.*

Right eye (in white):

1. Sc 6 in a magic ring (6)
2. Sc 4, inc x 2, change to black (8)
3. In BLO, sc 3, dc-inc x 2, inc, sc, inc (12)
4. Sc, hdc-inc, sc. FO

Belt buckle (in black):

1. Sc 6 in a magic circle, change to red (6)
2. In BLO [sc, inc] 3 times (9)
3. FO with a long tail. Sew a line down the middle before attaching to belt. You can also embroider the white eyes now too. Attach to front of belt.

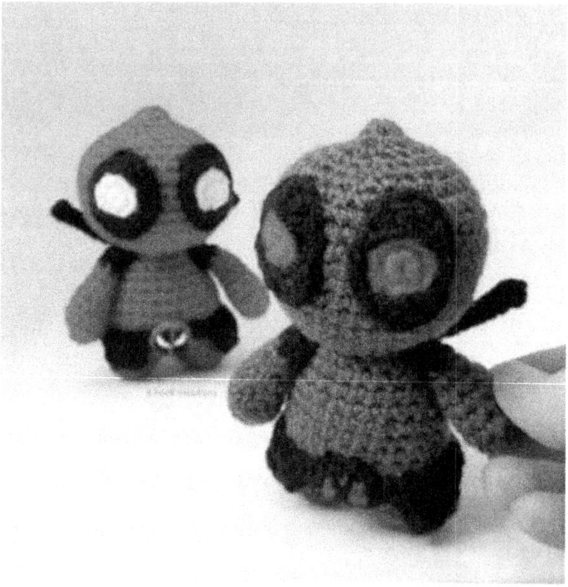

Super Heroes Crochet Ideas

If you want to make an XForce version, swap out dark gray for the red yarn and use red for the pupils instead of white. For the belt buckle, start with red and change to black for the 2nd row and make an 'X' with the tail of the black yarn.

Super Heroes Crochet Ideas

Printed in Great Britain
by Amazon